Storylines...

Picture sequences for language practice

Mark Fletcher and David Birt

Longman

London and New York

The authors express their admiration for the work being done by those voluntary organisations which try to relieve human suffering in many parts of the world, and also those which try to protect endangered animals (see sequences 11 and 16). A portion of the authors' royalties will be given to support such organisations.

Longman Group UK Limited,
Longman House, Burnt Mill, Harlow,
Essex CM20 2JE, England
and Associated Companies throughout the world.

Published in the United States of America by Longman Inc., New York

© Longman Group Limited 1983

First published 1983
Reprinted 1986
ISBN 0-582-79103-0

Set in 10/12pt Linotron 202 Century Schoolbook
Produced by Longman Singapore Publishers (Pte) Ltd.
Printed in Singapore.

Contents

Introduction and notes for the teacher.

Storylines consists of twenty picture sequences, each one depicting a story of immediate and contemporary appeal (conservation, sport, fashion, technology, natural disasters, charity work, humour and human interest), plus full exploitation material. The picture sequences are of four distinct types: comic, narrative, documentary and photographic, each with its own style of illustration.

Because of the subject matter *Storylines* is suitable for adult and for secondary students. The range of exploitation material prompts both oral work and written work. The exercises lead from controlled learning stages to freer practice stages. The types of exercise make the book very useful for those working towards the ARELS exam.

Part 1: Picture Sequences 1–10

Level and exploitation

These sequences are elementary/lower intermediate level. The list below shows the basic grammatical knowledge required to complete the exploitation material.

1 High Noon – simple present, simple past and present progressive
2 Tycoon – simple present
3 Hong Kong – simple present
4 Volcano – simple past
5 Reunion – simple past and past progressive
6 Bank Robbers – simple past and past progressive
7 International Report: Iceland and Cuba – comparatives and simple past
8 Fashions – comparatives and present perfect
9 Jogging – simple past and past progressive
10 Football Match – simple past

Using the stories

It is useful to start by letting the class look through the story, working in pairs or small groups. They can pool their understanding of the vocabulary provided. Then they should be in a position to move on to exercise A.

Exercise A: Questions

Apart from a few short-form answers to help build the students' confidence initially, the majority of the answers required are all simple sentences. These check understanding of the story and of the vocabulary, and practise grammatical accuracy. They can be answered orally 'round the class' either with or without preparation. For less able classes, it is advised that the students carefully prepare the answers in pairs.

Exercises B and C: Tell the story (1) and (2)

These exercises help build up a feeling for the structure of English, and help reinforce newly acquired skills and vocabulary. They give the students practice in manipulating a restricted number of elements in each story. The format in these exercises varies: filling in the missing word; putting sentences in order; completing the dialogue; correcting errors of fact; and matching the halves of split sentences. The class will need time to prepare these, working either individually or in pairs. The teacher can then ask for oral answers, or, with more able classes, a written version of the completed exercises.

Exercise D: Guided interview

The aim of this exercise is to achieve grammatical accuracy in asking and answering five or six simple questions within a realistic context. The resulting short dialogue can then be practised aloud by students working in pairs.

Exercise E: Tell the story (3)

After the previous tightly controlled exercises, students should be familiar with the content of the story. The next stage is to use the skills and material learnt, this time telling the story in the person of one of the characters from the story. The students should be given time to look through the story again. Their oral version will need monitoring to check that it includes words and phrases from the Vocabulary and the exercises Tell the story (1) and (2).

Exercise F: Writing

The short writing exercises give scope for greater freedom of expression, yet they are closely linked to the story and the previous exercises to provide plenty of help for the students.

Part 2: Picture Sequences 11–20

Level and exploitation

These units are suitable for lower intermediate/intermediate levels of English. A wider range of tenses is used, the exploitation is more 'stretching', and in some cases the subject matter is more difficult. The list below shows the basic grammatical knowledge needed to complete the exploitation material.

11 Ivory Poachers – simple present and present progressive, and present perfect
12 Protest! – simple present and present progressive, present perfect and first conditional
13 The Dinner Party – simple past
14 Athlete – simple present, simple past and 'has to/had to'
15 Vaccine – simple past, present perfect and simple future
16 Mother Theresa – simple present, simple past and simple future
17 Campers – simple past, 'going to' future, and 'must have/might have'
18 Balloon Flight – simple past and present perfect
19 The Microchip Revolution – present perfect, simple future and future passive
20 The Temples That Were Moved – simple past and past passive

Using the stories

The exploitation material for the second ten stories is more demanding than for the first ten, although the general approach to the stories remains the same.

Exercise A: Questions

Within the same framework as Part 1, some questions demanding slightly longer answers are occasionally introduced.

Exercises B and C: Tell the story (1) and (2)

A new element of 'rewriting the captions' is introduced sometimes for Tell the story (1). Thereafter the student is asked in exercise C to tell the story again without a second controlled practice stage. (Thus exercise C in Part 2 is roughly the same as exercise E in Part 1.)

Exercise D: Guided interview

This remains much the same as for Part 1.

Exercise E: Task

This new element is a communication activity designed for groups. It includes interviewing, establishing priorities, and sharing ideas. A short preparation time of 5–10 minutes is usually needed, and at the end there is often a 'report back' stage to the whole class. The Task for 'Microchip Revolution' is more lengthy than the others.

Exercise F: Writing

This follows naturally from the story or the Task, or both, so that familiar material can be reworked by students, using their imagination to develop it. Introductory questions give the students initial guidance. This Writing exercise can equally well be done after the Discussion, possibly as homework.

Exercise G: Discussion

For this, conversation is triggered off either by a number of leading questions for comment, or by a short 'pooling-of-ideas' activity to provide material for comparison.

General note

The topical nature of the stories means that they integrate well with project work exploring wide themes – especially where this uses magazine and newspaper articles, or listening material from newscasts.

High Noon

KILLER CLINT'S IN TOWN!

Vocabulary

Picture 1 a gunfighter, a bandit, a moustache
    2 a sheriff, a cowboy
    3 to be frightened, to run away
    4 to kick, a saloon
    5 to hide, a barman
    6 a shadow

A Questions

1 Can you describe Clint?
2 Did Clint look very happy when he arrived in Desertville?
3 Was the sheriff in the bar when Clint arrived?
4 Was everyone pleased to see him?
5 What did the people do?
6 Did Clint go to the sheriff's office as soon as he arrived?
7 Do you think Clint paid for his drinks?
8 What time did Clint go to find the sheriff?
9 What did the sheriff do when he saw Clint?
10 What do you think happened?

B Tell the story (1)

Cowboy:	Killer Clint is in town!	
Sheriff:	Where is he?	
Cowboy:		(picture 1)
Sheriff:	What's happening now?	
Cowboy:		(picture 3)
Sheriff:	Where's he going?	
Cowboy:		(picture 4)
Sheriff:	What's he ...?	
Cowboy:		(picture 5)
Sheriff:	What ...?	
Cowboy:		(picture 6)
Sheriff:	HELP!	

8

C   Tell the story (2)

Killer Clint is a very dangerous _gun_. He always
carried two guns. He always looks _dangerous_. He never
smile. Yesterday morning he _came_ _from_ the train
at Desertville. Everyone in the town was _frightened_.
People _run_ away. Clint _____ open the door of the
_____. The _____ gave him several large _____. At
_____ o'clock, Clint _____ the bar and _____
towards the _____ _____.

D   Guided interview

Ask the sheriff some questions.

For example: Ask him why he is hiding in his office.
                'Why are you hiding in your office?'
                'Because I'm frightened of Clint.'

1   Ask him why he is frightened of Clint.
2   Ask him where Clint is at the moment.

3   Ask him what the other people in the town are
     doing.
4   Ask him what Clint is going to do.
5   Ask him what *he* is going to do.

E   Tell the story (3)

Look at the pictures again. You are Killer Clint. Tell
the story in your own words. Try to use all the
vocabulary given.

F   Writing

Either   Write five sentences about picture 6.
    or   Write a newspaper article for the 'Desertville
            Star'. Describe Clint. What did he do? Why
            was everyone frightened? What happened at
            the end of the visit? Say what you think of
            the sheriff.

Tycoon

Sales reports and meetings 3.00–5.00 p.m.

Vocabulary

Picture 1 to wake up, a tray
    2 a chauffeur, a briefcase, servants
    3 a Rolls Royce, a doorman, to salute, an office block
    4 a meeting, chairman
    5 a chart, sales figures
    6 to entertain, customers, a night club, a cabaret, bags under the eyes, to enjoy oneself
    7 a mansion
    8 to be exhausted, to be tired out

A Questions

1 What does James have for breakfast?
2 How does he go to work?
3 Does he have meetings every morning?
4 What does he do in the afternoons?
5 Is business good?
6 What does he do every evening?
7 Where does he take his customers?
8 Why does he look so tired?
9 What is good and what is bad about his life?
10 What do you think he is going to do tomorrow?

B Tell the story (1)

Put these phrases in the right order to tell the story.

a In the afternoons, he looks at the sales reports.
b He gets home very late.
c They have dinner and watch the cabaret.
d The next day he gets up at the same time and does the same things.
e James is a millionaire and he lives in a large mansion.
f In the evenings he entertains important customers.
g He has champagne and boiled eggs for breakfast every day.
h His chauffeur drives him to work in a Rolls Royce.
i Every morning he holds important meetings.
j He leaves the house at 7.00 a.m.

The next day...

C Tell the story (2)

James Cash is a very rich man. He is 35 years old and he is _____ of a big company. Every day he _____ breakfast in bed _____ 6 a.m. He has _____ and _____ _____ for breakfast. He also _____ phone calls and reads _____ at breakfast time. Then he gets dressed. He always wears a smart _____ to the office. His _____ help him.

At 7.00 his chauffeur _____ him _____ his office. He has business _____ every morning. Every afternoon he _____ _____ the sales reports. Sales go _____ every year because business is good.

In the evenings he _____ important _____. They go to a night club. They have dinner and watch the _____. At 2 o'clock in the _____, his chauffeur drives him _____. He goes to bed. He is always _____. The next day is exactly the same!

D Guided interview

Ask James Cash some questions.

For example: Ask him if he is very rich.
               'Are you very rich?'
               'Yes, I am.'

1   Ask him where he lives.
2   Ask him about his work.
3   Ask him how he gets to work.
4   Ask him if he often looks at sales reports.
5   Ask him what he does in the evenings.
6   Ask him if business is good.
7   Ask him why he is tired.
8   Ask him if he is happy.

E Tell the story (3)

Look at the pictures again. You are James Cash. Describe your daily routine in your own words. Talk about your house, your job, and the way you spend your time. Try to use all the vocabulary given.

F Writing

You are James. Write a page in your diary about yesterday. Begin 'Yesterday morning I woke up at...'

International Report: Hong Kong

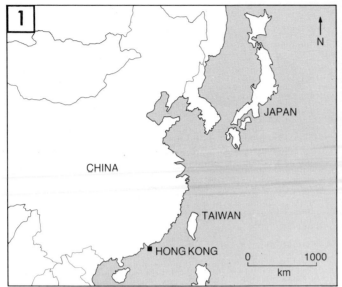

Area – 1000 sq. km.
Population – 4.5 million

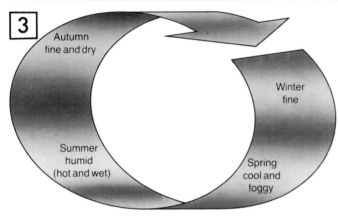

Autumn
fine and dry

Winter
fine

Summer
humid
(hot and wet)

Spring
cool and
foggy

4 million tourists a year

Vocabulary

Picture 1 an island
    2 blocks of flats, skyscrapers, crowded
    3 the weather, the climate
    4 Kai Tak airport
    5 a factory, to manufacture
    6 a harbour
    7 to trade with
    8 duty-free, jade figures

A Questions

1 Where is Hong Kong?
2 How many people live there?
3 How big is it?
4 What's the weather like in autumn?
5 How many tourists visit it each year?
6 Are there a lot of factories in Hong Kong?
7 What things does Hong Kong make and export?
8 What areas does Hong Kong trade with?
9 What things do tourists buy?
10 Why is it a good place for shopping?

B Tell the story (1)

Hong Kong is an _____. It is near _____. It is about _____ _____ from Japan. Over 4 million people _____ there, so it is very _____. There are a lot of _____ _____ _____ and a lot of _____ in the city. The people _____ two languages, Cantonese and English. The climate is very _____ and _____ in summer. It is fine in winter. Every year about _____ million _____ visit Hong Kong. The main industries are _____ _____ and _____. There are a lot of _____ in Hong Kong which manufacture these products. Another very important _____ is tourism.

In Hong Kong's harbour you can see _____ from many different parts of the _____. Hong Kong _____ with America, Asia, Australia and many other areas.

Four million _____ visit Hong Kong every year. Typical souvenirs are _____ and _____. These are _____-_____ so they are very cheap. You can also _____ made-to-measure _____ and beautiful _____ _____.

12

Main exports – electronic equipment, textiles, plastics.

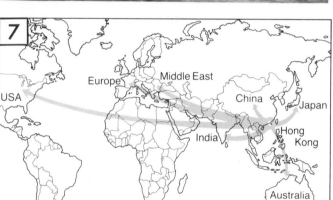

C Tell the story (2)

Correct all the mistakes, which are in italics, and write out this description of Hong Kong.

Hong Kong is a small *village in the mountains*. It is in *South America* and it is *200* km from *Mexico*. *Not many* people live there so it is very *quiet*. A lot of people work *on farms* and they make textiles and plastic products. Plastic products from Hong Kong are very *expensive*. *Not many* tourists come to Hong Kong because it's beautiful and a good place for shopping. Ships from all over the world come to the big *airport*. They bring *textiles and electronic equipment* to Hong Kong and they take *food and oil* to other countries.

D Guided interview

Interview the receptionist at a Hong Kong hotel.

For example: Ask her where she works.
'Where do you work?'
'I work in a hotel.'

1 Ask her if many tourists come to Hong Kong.
2 Ask her what things Hong Kong exports.
3 Ask her what the tourists buy.
4 Ask her why Hong Kong is such a good place for shopping.
5 Ask her if she likes working in Hong Kong and why.

E Tell the story (3)

Look at the pictures again and talk about Hong Kong in your own words. Try to use all the vocabulary given.

F Writing

Imagine that last month you went to Hong Kong for a holiday. Write a short letter to a friend. Describe your visit. Did you like Hong Kong? What was the weather like? What did you see? Did you buy any souvenirs?

Volcano

Clouds of volcanic ash shoot upwards from Mount Saint Helens in the state of Washington, USA.

The eruption causes mudslides which cover a huge area.

The mud blocks rivers which flood, trapping animals and men.

Vocabulary

Picture 1   to erupt, an eruption, lava
    2   mud, to flow
    3   to flood, floods, to escape
    4   a helicopter, a survivor, to treat injuries, burns
    5   to examine, a farmer, crops, volcanic ash, to ruin
    6   a salesman, car stickers, to make money

A   Questions

1   What is happening in picture 1?
2   Does a volcanic eruption cause a lot of damage?
3   What happened to the river when the mud flowed into it?
4   What are the men in picture 3 trying to do?
5   Why is it dangerous?
6   How did the survivor injure his hand?
7   What is the doctor doing?
8   Why is the farmer very worried?
9   How is one man making money out of the eruption?
10   When did these particular eruptions occur?

B   Tell the story (1)

What's on the news?

18 May 1980

'Here is the news. A _____ called Mount Saint Helens is _____ in the state of Washington. Clouds of volcanic _____ are rising into the sky. _____ and mud are covering the area around the volcano. The River Toutle _____ _____. Horses and other animals are in danger from the _____. People _____ _____ to safety. Helicopters are searching for _____ of the disaster. The latest news is that a helicopter has picked up a survivor with serious _____. A doctor in the helicopter_____ _____ the survivor's _____.'

26 May 1980

'Here is some more news of the volcanic eruptions at Mount Saint Helens. In the last week tons of _____ _____ have fallen on the _____ around the volcano. Farmers are very _____. A lot of ash can _____ their _____.

But some local people are _____ _____ from the eruption. One _____ is _____ souvenir stickers to tourists in the disaster area.'

14

A helicopter rescue of a survivor badly burnt
by the lava.

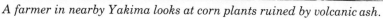

A farmer in nearby Yakima looks at corn plants ruined by volcanic ash.

Making the best of the disaster.

C Tell the story (2)

Rewrite these sentences in the correct order to tell the
story of the eruption.

a A lot of people were rescued by helicopters.
b The lava and mudflows caused rivers to flood.
c When the volcano erupted there was a great
  cloud of volcanic ash above Mount Saint Helens.
d But some people made money out of the disaster.
e After the eruption, ash fell over a wide area.
f They sold stickers about the eruption.
g The rising water trapped people and animals.
h Then lava began to flow out of the volcano.
i The farmers were worried because the ash ruined
  their crops.

D Guided interview

Interview a farmer who lives near the volcano.

For example: Ask him what happened when the
              volcano erupted.
              'What happened when the volcano
              erupted?'
              'Clouds of volcanic ash rose into the
              air.'

1 Ask him if he saw any lava.
2 Ask him if any ash fell on his fields.
3 Ask him how much damage there was.
4 Ask him why a lot of animals died.
5 Ask him if many people were hurt.
6 Ask him if anyone did well out of the eruption.

E Tell the story (3)

Now look at the photographs again. You live near the
volcano. Tell the story in your own words. Try to use
all the vocabulary given.

F Writing

You are a journalist. Use these notes to write a report
of the Mount Saint Helens eruption.

– 4.30 a.m., 18 May 1980
– smoke/tons of ash
– lava/mud
– River Toutle
– people/animals
– ash/crops
– tourists

Reunion

Vocabulary

Picture 1 granddaughter
    2 a travel agent
    3 an in-flight film/movie, an air hostess
    5 to kiss, to make a mistake
    6 to be embarrassed
    7 to take notes
    8 to explain

A Questions

1 Who did the old man get a letter from?
2 Why did he want to go to Canada?
3 How did he go there?
4 What did he do during the flight?
5 What was the weather like when he arrived in Ottawa?
6 What did he do in the arrival lounge?
7 Why did he make a mistake?
8 How did he feel at that moment?
9 What was happening when the granddaughter arrived?
10 What happened when the granddaughter arrived?

B Tell the story (1)

An old man _____ a letter from his granddaughter who lives in _____. While he was reading the _____, he had an idea. He decided to _____ to Canada to _____ her. So he _____ a ticket for Canada.

He _____ from London to Ottawa. While he was _____ in the plane, he watched an _____-_____ _____, and _____ several meals. The _____ took seven hours.

When he _____ to Ottawa, it was cold and it was _____. He looked for his _____. He went _____ the arrival lounge and _____ a woman there. She _____ _____ a black _____ and a fur _____. He thought it _____ his granddaughter, and he kissed her. The _____ wasn't his granddaughter, so she was very _____ ! She _____ a policeman. While the _____ was talking to the old man, the granddaughter _____. She was also wearing a _____ _____ and a _____ _____. She kissed the _____ _____. Everyone was _____ again.

C Tell the story (2)

Complete the conversation by choosing the best alternative word.

Woman: Hi, officer!

Policeman: Yes, miss. What's the *trouble/mistake*?

Woman: This man has just *hit/kissed* me!

Policeman: Is he a *friend/son* of yours?

Woman: I've never *seen/spoken/known* him before in my life.

Old man: Officer, I'm *stupid/unhappy/afraid* I made a mistake.

Policeman: Give me your name and *number/address/licence*.

Old man: I'm just *visiting/flying/looking* for a month to see my granddaughter.

Grand-daughter: Hello, grandpa! How lovely to *see/hear/kiss* you again!

Policeman: Is this man *really/soon/often* your grandfather?

Grand-daughter: *Now/sometimes/certainly* he is! He's coming to *return/stay/leave* in Chesterville.

D Guided interview

Interview the other woman in the arrival lounge.

For example: Ask her why she was in the arrival lounge.
'Why were you in the arrival lounge?'
'I was there to meet some friends.'

1 Ask her what she was wearing.
2 Ask her why she called a policeman.
3 Ask her to describe the old man.
4 Ask her what the policeman did.
5 Ask her what happened next.

E Tell the story (3)

Look at the pictures again. You are the old man's granddaughter. Tell your part of the story. Use as much of the vocabulary given as you can.

F Writing

You are the airport policeman. Write a report of the incident in the arrival lounge. Begin 'At half past ten on Tuesday morning I was ...'

Bank Robbers

Vocabulary

Picture 1 a robbery, masks, a cashier
      2 to guard, to film, a camera
      3 to look for clues, fingerprints, a magnifying glass, to interview witnesses
      5 to relax, a luxurious villa
      6 to arrest
      7 handcuffs

A Questions

1 Were there any customers in the bank?
2 What did they do when the robbers came in?
3 How many robbers were there?
4 What were the robbers wearing?
5 Did they all look the same?
6 Where was the camera in the bank?
7 How did the detectives start to investigate the robbery?
8 Why didn't the robbers enjoy themselves for very long?
9 What were the robbers doing when the police arrived?
10 What do you think will happen to the robbers?

B Tell the story (1)

Put these sentences in order.
a They stole a lot of money and then got away in a car.
b They watched the film and identified the robbers.
c They were relaxing in the sun at a luxurious villa.
d While the police were looking for them, the robbers were enjoying themselves.
e Three men came into the bank with guns.
f Detectives interviewed the customers.
g They arrested the men and put them into a police van.
h They were wearing masks.
i The police rushed in.
j They didn't notice that a camera was filming them.

C Tell the story (2)

Three men robbed a _____. They were _____ masks and they _____ guns. While one of them took the _____, another one _____ the door and the third one pointed his gun at the _____. He ordered the frightened customers to _____ their _____ in the air.

The robbers didn't notice a hidden _____ which
_____ _____ them. They ran out of the _____ with
the _____.

The _____ came to the bank and _____ the
customers. They _____ for fingerprints and they
_____ the film of the robbery. While the police _____
_____ for them, the robbers _____ _____
themselves. They _____ _____ in a large villa with a
_____ _____ in the garden. One day the _____
rushed in and _____ them. They _____ them into a
_____ _____. The _____ will go to prison.

D Guided interview

Interview one of the girls who was with the robbers at
the villa.

For example: Ask her if she knew the men were
robbers.
'Did you know the men were robbers?'
'Of course not. I thought they were
very nice.'

1 Ask her where she met the men.
2 Ask her when they came to the villa.
3 Ask her if the men gave her expensive presents.

4 Ask her what they were doing when the police
arrived.
5 Ask her how she feels now.

E Tell the story (3)

Look at the pictures again. You are one of the robbers.
Tell the story in your own words. Try to use all the
vocabulary given.

F Writing

Eight words from the picture story are hidden in this
letter block. One of the words is ringed. The words are
all in straight lines, including diagonals. Find the
other seven words and then use each one in a separate
sentence.

C	R	G	N	O	P	R	D	P
A	C	U	S	T	O	M	E	R
M	B	N	M	C	L	Q	X	I
E	U	A	T	F	I	L	M	S
R	I	L	N	A	C	R	U	O
A	M	A	S	K	E	B	S	N

International Report: Iceland and Cuba

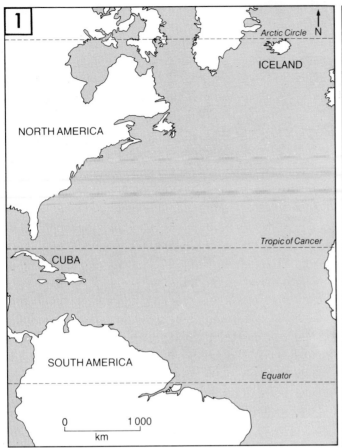

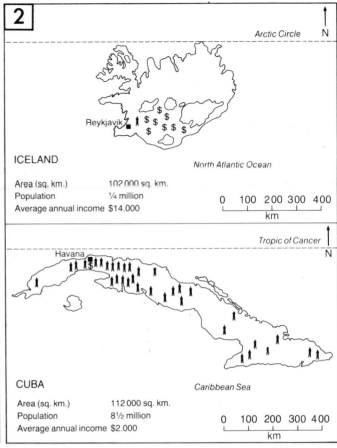

Vocabulary

Picture 1   the equator
    2   size, length
    3   the weather, the climate
    4   sugar cane, sugar plantations, rum
    5   fishing, a geyser

A   Questions

1   Is Iceland nearer the Arctic Circle or the Tropic of Cancer?
2   How big is Cuba?
3   How many people live in Iceland?
4   Can you compare:
    a   the size of the populations of Cuba and Iceland?
    b   their average incomes?
    c   their distances from the equator?
    d   their rainfall?
    e   their temperatures in January and June?
5   Can you name two things that are produced in Cuba?
6   What is the main industry in Iceland?

B   Tell the story (1)

Ten sentences have each been split up into two halves. Find the correct halves (one from each group) and write the sentences out.

1   People in Iceland wear
2   Many Cubans work
3   Iceland is smaller
4   You can see geysers
5   Cuba is
6   In Cuba there are more people
7   Rum is not
8   In Cuba you can swim
9   Many Icelanders are employed as
10   The Cubans are poorer

a   larger than Iceland.
b   than Cuba.
c   most of the year.
d   in the sugar plantations.
e   produced in Iceland.
f   warm clothing.
g   deep-sea fishermen.
h   in Iceland.
i   than the Icelanders.
j   than in Iceland.

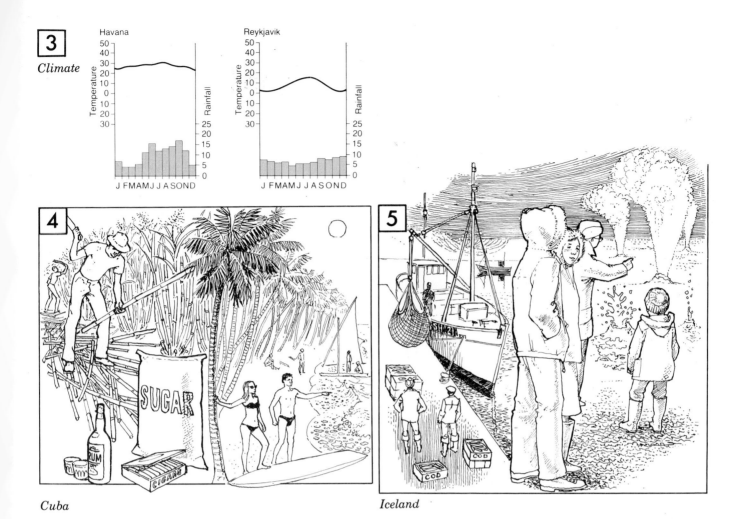

3 *Climate*

Havana

Reykjavik

Cuba

Iceland

C Tell the story (2)

A journalist wrote a report about Cuba and Iceland, but he made a lot of mistakes. Rewrite his report, correcting all the errors of fact, which are in italics.

Cuba is *smaller* than Iceland and *nearer to* Britain. The Cubans are *richer* than the Icelanders, and they live in a *cooler* climate. Iceland is *wetter* than Cuba and the main industry is *sugar production*. The *huge* population of Iceland live mainly in the capital in the *north* of the island. Tourists go to Iceland to see the *palm trees*. It is so *warm* there that they wear *few* clothes when sightseeing. This is because Iceland is so *far from* the Arctic Circle.

D Guided interview

Interview a tourist who has recently returned from *either* Iceland *or* Cuba.

For example: Ask him what time of year he went there.
'What time of year did you go there?'
'I went there in spring.'

1 Ask him how he travelled.
2 Ask him what the climate was like.
3 Ask him what interesting things he saw.
4 Ask him what he enjoyed doing.
5 Ask him what he didn't like.
6 Ask him for some details about the size of the country and its population.

E Tell the story (3)

Look at the pictures again and talk about Iceland and Cuba in your own words. Try to use all the vocabulary given.

F Writing

Make a list of six ways in which your own country is different from either Iceland or Cuba. Write one or two sentences explaining whether you would prefer to spend a month in Iceland or Cuba – or in your own country.

Fashions

A Victorian gentleman and his wife pose
for the camera in 1860.

The latest thing in tennis wear,
1880.

The smart set at a 1925 tennis tournament.

Vocabulary

Picture 1   a jacket, a dress, a cane, a watch-chain, a
crease, formal
     2   frills, a racquet, a blazer, a striped cap
     3   fur trimming, a collar, flannel trousers
     4   a suit, an overcoat
     5   a mini-skirt, a cravat, patterned
     6   jeans, corduroy, unisex clothes, casual
clothes.

A   Questions

1   Are the clothes in picture 1 more formal or less
formal than the clothes in picture 6?
2   Which is better for tennis: modern sports clothes
or the clothes in picture 2?
3   What are the fashion differences between the
clothes in pictures 1 and 3?
4   Are the clothes in picture 4 smarter than or not
so smart as the clothes in picture 5?
5   What have been the biggest changes in fashion
since 1860?
6   Have there been any important changes in
materials?
7   Have there been any important changes in the
way clothes are made?
8   Which of the ladies' dresses is the prettiest?
9   Which two men's fashions do you like best?
10   What do the changes in these fashions tell us
about changes in the way of life?

B   Tell the story (1)

Choose the correct alternative from the words in
italics.

In Victorian times, clothes were more *casual/formal*
than they are now. Men wore *heavy/light* jackets and
trousers with *no/neat* creases. Ladies wore very full
skirts/cravats, which became *tighter/looser* in the
1880s. Their sporting clothes were very
similar/different to ordinary clothes. But men wore
striped *blazers/shoes* and caps for tennis.

In the 1920s, clothes were much *looser/tighter*
fitting. The 'Flappers' sometimes wore expensive coats
trimmed with *fur/creases*. Twenty years *earlier/later*,
suits were in fashion for both men and women. The
women's jackets had a rather *baggy/military* style,
called the 'New Look'.

By the end of the 'Swinging Sixties', many
men/women were wearing miniskirts. Men's clothing
became more *colourful/dull* and *unusual/Victorian*.
Ten years later, men's and women's clothes were very
similar/different. This style was called *unisex/
feminine*. It was the age of *blue jeans/dinner jackets*.

C   Tell the story (2)

Ten sentences have each been split into two halves.
Find the correct halves (one from each column) and
write the sentences out.

An American soldier offers gifts, 1945.

Relaxing in the King's Road, London, in 1967.

Street scene, Europe, 1980.

1 Clothing was very formal
2 Victorian ladies wore
3 In the 1880s, men wore
4 The 'Flappers' had loose-fitting
5 In 1945, women's suits had
6 In the 'Swinging Sixties'
7 Men's clothing became
8 By 1980, many men and women
9 This fashion was called
10 Fashion has changed many times

a unisex.
b striped blazers for tennis.
c a military look.
d wore jeans.
e long skirts for tennis.
f more colourful.
g since 1860.
h in Victorian times.
i miniskirts were introduced.
j dresses.

D Interview

Make a grid like the one on the right. Then interview any student or member of staff. Find out their opinions about the clothes in the photographs.

For example: 'Which of the styles for men do you think is the most comfortable?'
'I think the one in picture 1 is the most comfortable.'

Fill in their opinions for all the boxes.

name	most comfortable	most practical	most elegant	most fun to wear
styles for men				
styles for women				

E Tell the story (3)

Look at the photographs again. Work in pairs. You are fashion designers. Choose *one* picture and work out a description of the fashions for men and women for that period. Tell your description to the rest of the class beginning 'This year fashions are . . .'. Try to use all the vocabulary given. The rest of the class guesses the period you are talking about.

F Writing

In England, April 1st is the day for practical jokes. Produce a serious-sounding newspaper article to persuade teenage boys or girls to adopt a really crazy fashion. Date your article 'April 1st' and think up a suitable headline.

Jogging

Vocabulary

Picture 1   a mirror, to look at oneself, a stomach
     2   to get fit, to put on, shorts, a running vest
     3   to go jogging, to sweat
     4   a street corner
     5   to trip over, a lead, to hurt oneself
     6   to get up
     7   to limp
     8   to be soaked through, waste paper basket

A   Questions

1. Is Tony slim or rather fat?
2. Why did Tony go jogging?
3. What did he wear for the run?
4. Why did the boys laugh at him?
5. Why was the dog sitting there on the road?
6. Why did Tony's arm hurt?
7. Did the dog's owner apologise?
8. What else went wrong on the run?
9. How did Tony feel when he got home?
10. What did he do?

B   Tell the story (1)

Tony looked at himself in the _____. He was quite _____. He had a big _____. He _____ his 'Keep Fit' book and decided to get fit. He put on a _____ and _____.

He ran along the road. Some boys _____ at him because he was running so _____. Two ladies _____ _____ on the pavement. One of them had a _____. Tony _____ _____ the dog's lead. While he was _____ _____, the dog bit him. Its owner got very _____ with Tony. While he _____ _____ home, it started to rain and he got very _____.

He stood in his room feeling_____. He was wet and he had a backache. He had a cut on his _____ and he had a _____ on his arm. He _____ the 'Keep Fit' book into the _____ _____ _____.

C   Tell the story (2)

Complete this dialogue, from Tony's point of view.

Why did you go jogging?
Tony: Because I was too fat.

Did you enjoy your keep fit run?
Tony:
Why not?
Tony:
Why did they laugh at you?
Tony:
How did you cut your knee?
Tony:
What are those red marks on your arm?
Tony:
Why have you got a bad cold?
Tony:
Are you going for another run tomorrow?
Tony:
Can I borrow your 'Keep Fit' book, please?
Tony:

D   Guided interview

Interview the owner of the dog.

For example: Ask her what the dog was doing when
Tony ran round the corner.

'What was the dog doing when Tony ran round
the corner?'
'It was sitting quietly on the road.'

1   Ask her if it is usually a friendly dog, or if it often
attacks people.
2   Ask her why it bit Tony.
3   Ask her if Tony was badly hurt.
4   Ask her why she didn't apologise to Tony.
5   Ask her if she will punish the dog.

E   Tell the story (3)

Look at the pictures again. You are Tony. Tell us all
about your keep fit run yesterday. Try to use all the
vocabulary given.

F   Writing

You are Tony's wife. Write a letter to the newspaper
about jogging. Describe what happened to your
husband on his first jog. Mention some other ways of
keeping fit which would be better.

Football Match

Vocabulary

Picture 2 to get tickets, a stadium
  3 to cheer
  4 to score a goal
  5 the second half, a foul, an injury, the referee
  6 a penalty, to make a save
  8 to prepare supper
  9 a replay, a recording

A Questions

1 What did Jim and his father do on Saturday?
2 When did the game start?
3 Why did the crowd cheer?
4 What happened in the second half?
5 What did the referee do?
6 Why didn't Munich score from the penalty?
7 What was the result of the game?
8 Was the crowd pleased?
9 What did Jim and his father do when they got home?
10 Do you think Jim's mother is keen on football?

B Tell the story (1)

Rewrite these sentences in the correct order to tell what happened.

a In the second half there was a foul.
b Jim's mother was not pleased.
c The goalkeeper saved the penalty.
d They arrived at the stadium at ten to three.
e Liverpool won one–nil.
f They watched a recording of the game.
g They took their supper and switched on the TV.
h Liverpool scored at twenty-five past three.
i Jim and his father decided to go to a football match.
j They got home at half past six.

C Tell the story (2)

One Saturday Jim and his father decided to _____ to a football match between Liverpool and Munich. They _____ _____ the stadium at ten to three. The players came onto the _____ and the game started.

26

It was very _____. At _____-_____ _____ _____ Liverpool scored a goal. The crowd _____. In the _____ _____ there was a foul by a Liverpool defender. The referee _____ a _____ to Munich. The Liverpool goalkeeper _____ the penalty. The Munich players were very disappointed. Liverpool _____ the game one−nil.

Jim and his father left the _____ feeling happy. They _____ _____ at half past six. Jim's mother was cooking in the _____. Jim and his father put their supper on a _____ and went into the sitting room. They _____ on the TV and watched a _____ of the Liverpool/Munich game. Jim's mother was not pleased.

D Guided interview

Interview the captain of the Liverpool football team.

For example: Ask him if Liverpool were playing at home or away.

'Were Liverpool playing at home or away?'
'We were playing at home.'

1 Ask him which side scored the first goal.
2 Ask him what happened in the second half.
3 Ask him if the referee was right to give a penalty.
4 Ask him what he thinks about the Liverpool goalkeeper.
5 Ask him how the team will celebrate.

E Tell the story (3)

Look at the pictures again. You are Jim. Tell us what happened on Saturday. Try to use all the vocabulary given.

F Writing

Write a short report about any sporting event you have seen. Where was it? Who was playing? Was it exciting? Who won? Were you pleased with the result?

Ivory Poachers

Vocabulary

Picture 2   elephants, poachers, automatic rifles, to hunt, tusks
      3   game wardens, binoculars, a Land Rover
      4   a shoot-out, the bush
      5   statistics, a fine

A   Questions

1   Has the amount of poaching changed during the last twenty years?
2   Why do the poachers hunt elephants?
3   How do the poachers kill the elephants?
4   What do they do next?
5   What happens when the wardens find a gang of poachers?
6   Why is the game wardens' job dangerous?
7   How are poachers punished when they are caught?
8   Where do the poachers operate?
9   How has the price of ivory changed since 1970?
10   How has the elephant population changed in Africa since 1960?

B   Tell the story (1)

Twenty years ago there were hundreds of thousands of elephants in East Africa. At that time, there were not many _____ and they only _____ a few hundred elephants each year. But since the wars of the 1970s, the number of well-armed poachers in East Africa has _____. They _____ the animals with _____ _____ and _____ _____ their tusks. When they have cut off the _____, they carry them away to _____ to ivory dealers.

Sometimes _____ _____ find the poachers and there is a _____. Usually the poachers _____ into the bush. Sometimes the wardens _____ them and take them to court, but the_____ for killing elephants is very small. Soon the poachers are killing again.

In the _____ ten years, poachers have _____ approximately 40,000 elephants in Zambia, 30,000 in the Central African Republic and _____ in Uganda. Poachers have also killed _____ game wardens in the last five years. During this time the price of ivory _____ _____. Things made from _____ include carvings, billiard balls and piano keys.

Poaching has had a _____ effect on the numbers of elephants. These magnificient _____ may disappear completely from the game parks of _____ _____ if poaching is not _____.

28

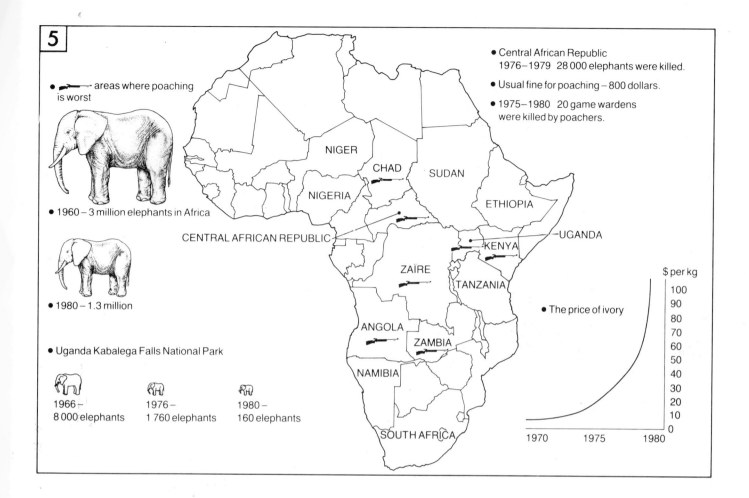

5

areas where poaching is worst

1960 – 3 million elephants in Africa

1980 – 1.3 million

Uganda Kabalega Falls National Park

1966 – 8 000 elephants   1976 – 1 760 elephants   1980 – 160 elephants

Central African Republic
1976–1979 28 000 elephants were killed.

Usual fine for poaching – 800 dollars.

1975–1980 20 game wardens were killed by poachers.

The price of ivory

$ per kg

NIGER, CHAD, SUDAN, NIGERIA, ETHIOPIA, CENTRAL AFRICAN REPUBLIC, UGANDA, KENYA, ZAÏRE, TANZANIA, ANGOLA, ZAMBIA, NAMIBIA, SOUTH AFRICA

C Tell the story (2)

Look at the pictures again. You are a representative of the World Wildlife Fund. Use the pictures to summarize the situation in a short talk. Mention the numbers of elephants, where they live, why poaching has increased, and how you are trying to protect elephants from extinction.

D Guided interview

Interview a game warden.

For example: Ask him where he works.
'Where do you work?'
'I work in a game park in Uganda.'

1 Ask him about the numbers of elephants killed.
2 Ask him the reasons for poaching.
3 Ask him how the poachers kill the elephants.
4 Ask him about the punishments for poaching.
5 Ask him about the future of elephants.

Then interview an ivory dealer.

6 Ask him about the price of ivory.
7 Ask him what sort of people buy ivory, and why.
8 Ask him what he thinks about the ivory business and its effect on the future of elephants.

E Task

List five things that could be done to help save elephants from extinction.

F Writing

Seven words from the picture story are hidden in this letter block. The words are all in straight lines or diagonals. One of the words is ringed. Find the other six words, and then use each word in a different sentence.

```
P  Y  B  W  A  R  D  E  N
R  O  R  G  Z  X  R  N  O
Z (G  A  M  E  P  A  R  K)
L  O  U  C  T  C  S  U  T
E  L  E  P  H  A  N  T  U
B  S  M  R  O  E  M  K  S
Q  R  I  F  L  E  R  D  K
U  P  N  A  S  T  O  D  S
```

G Discussion

Is hunting popular in your country? What animals are hunted and why? Do hunters need a licence? Is there any poaching? Are any animals in danger of extinction?

Protest!

Nuclear plant 'crucial for UK survival'

Some people believe that we need nuclear power stations . . .

2

. . . like this

3

Other people are not so keen.

Vocabulary

Picture 1   to be crucial, survival
     2   a nuclear power station, a model
     3   a protest march
     4   an alternative source of energy, a windmill
     5   a site, a bulldozer
     6   a digger bucket, unemployment

A   Questions

1   Does 'crucial for survival' mean that Britain needs nuclear power, or not?
2   If the new power station is built, will it cover a large area or a small area?
3   What are the marchers carrying in picture 3?
4   What is their attitude to nuclear power?
5   What can the windmill in picture 4 do?
6   Where are the protesters in picture 5?
7   What are they doing?
8   In what age group are the protesters?
9   Are the protesters angry, or bored, or good-humoured?
10   Are the police angry, or bored, or good-humoured?

B   Tell the story (1)

Write out these captions, choosing the correct alternative from the words in italics.

1   Some industrialists believe that Britain will survive only if more *gas/nuclear* power stations are *built/discovered* to make electricity.
2   A *model/map* shows how the nuclear power station will *produce/appear* if it is built.
3   Protesters *run/march* through London, demanding that the nuclear programme is *stopped/extended*.
4   The protesters believe that the government should *destroy/examine* alternative sources of energy. Here scientists test a *new/sunny* device for using energy from the *waves/wind* to produce electricity.
5   Young protesters try to stop work at the *home/site* for the nuclear power station. If the bulldozer moves forward it *will/won't* crush them.
6   Soon protesters *occupy/leave* the whole site. Police arrive to tell the protesters to *leave/stay*. If the protesters refuse, they may be *rewarded/arrested*.

C   Tell the story (2)

Look at the photographs again. You are one of the protesters. Explain how you heard about the plans to build the power station. Say why you joined the protest campaign. Describe the march and the demonstration at the power station site.

The search for other forms of power continues.

Meanwhile down at the site for a nuclear power station . . .

. . . protesters find a new use for a digger bucket.

D Guided interview

Interview a policeman at the power station site.

For example: Ask him how long he has been a policeman.
'How long have you been a policeman?'
'I've been in the Police Force for six years.'

1 Ask him why he was called to the site.
2 Ask him what the weather was like.
3 Ask him what age most of the protesters were.
4 Ask him what the protesters shouted.
5 Ask him if the protesters were violent or peaceful.
6 Ask him what happened when he ordered the protesters to move.

E Task

Work in groups.

a Find out how many of your group are in favour of more nuclear power stations and how many are against.
b Find out which alternative energy sources people think are best.
c List four ways of saving energy.

Give your report to the class.

F Writing

You are a representative of British Nuclear Fuels. In a short written statement point out the advantages of nuclear power and some of the problems of alternative energy sources. Choose any three alternative energy sources from this list:

wind power
hydroelectric power
wave power
tide power
solar power
geothermal power

Think about availability, cost and efficiency, and their effect on the environment.

G Discussion

Forty years ago, a nuclear power station could not have been built. But now scientific progress has made this form of power possible. Form a group to make a list of the *good* results of scientific progress this century, and a list of the *bad* results. Discuss your lists with other groups, and try to reach agreement on the three most important good developments – and the three worst!

Vocabulary

Picture 1 to invite
    2 a salmon, a sauce
    3 to lay the table, a table cloth, cutlery
    4 to change, a suit, a long dress, jewellery
    5 to welcome, to introduce
    6 to be horrified
    7 to burst into tears, to cry, to rush out
    8 to look smug, pleased with oneself

A Questions

1 Why did Mr Smith ring up his friend, Mr Plummer?
2 What did Mr Smith do while his wife was cooking the sauce?
3 What did Mrs Smith prepare for the main course?
4 What did the Smiths wear for dinner?
5 What did the Plummers bring?
6 Why was everyone horrified when they saw the dinner table?
7 What did Mrs Smith do?
8 What did Mr Smith do?
9 Why did the cat look so pleased?
10 What do you think will happen to the cat?

B Tell the story (1)

Mr Smith decided to _____ Mr Plummer and invite him to _____. Mrs Smith spent a long time in the kitchen _____ dinner. The Smiths were very proud of the main dish, a _____ salmon.

They changed into their best _____ and went down to welcome their _____, the Plummers. When they all saw the _____ plate they were _____. Mrs Plummer comforted Mrs Smith, who was _____. Meanwhile Mr Smith ran to a shop and _____ some _____ and _____. During supper, the _____ looked very pleased with itself.

C Tell the story (2)

Look at the pictures again. You are Mr/Mrs Smith. Talk about the dinner party. Mention the invitation, the preparations, your reaction to the disaster — and what happened.

D Guided interview

Two of the class are Mr and Mrs Plummer. Ask them about the dinner party last Saturday.

32

For example: Ask them if they have been to dinner with the Smiths before.
'Have you ever been to dinner with the Smiths before?'
'No, we haven't. Last Saturday was the first time.'

1 Ask them why the evening was so unusual.
2 Ask them about Mrs Smith's reaction – and what they did about it.
3 Ask them whether they enjoyed the evening.
4 Ask them how the cat looked after its special dinner.
5 Ask them if they like animals and if they have any cats of their own.
6 Ask them whether they are planning to invite the Smiths to dinner soon.

E   Task

Here are nine captions for the pictures. Rewrite them in the correct order. Work in pairs.

A proud moment.
Welcoming the guests.
Mr Smith to the rescue.
An invitation by phone.
Preparations in the kitchen.
A smug cat.
A horrid surprise.
Changing for dinner.
Tears and comfort.

Now write your own caption for each picture.

F   Writing

Write a letter of thanks from Mrs Plummer to the Smiths.

Mention – your gratitude for the evening.
         – your enjoyment of the conversation.
         – your pleasure in having fish and chips for the first time in years.
         – your hope that the cat is not ill.

G   Discussion

Form a group to discuss the menu for a perfect dinner party. Have as many courses as you like, and as many wines and liqueurs. All the group must agree with each item. Write your final menu out.

Athlete

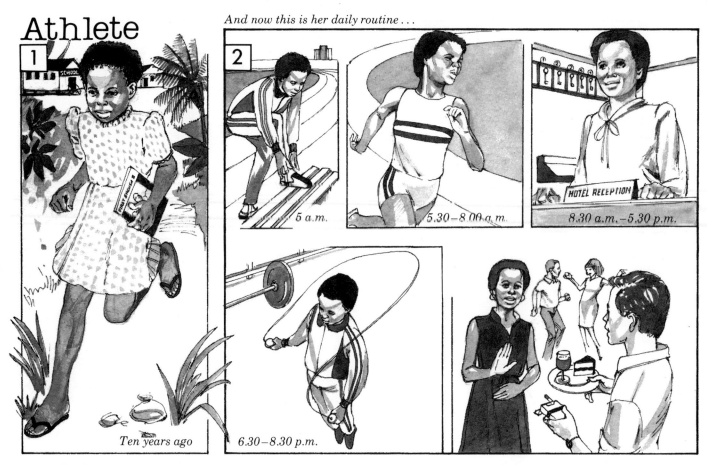

1 Ten years ago

And now this is her daily routine...

2 5 a.m.   5.30–8.00 a.m.   8.30 a.m.–5.30 p.m.   6.30–8.30 p.m.

Vocabulary

Picture 1 the jungle
2 running/training shoes, a track, to train, a receptionist, skipping, a gym, chocolates
3 a race, to line up for the start, a stadium
4 to cross the line, a close finish
5 a rostrum, a medal

A Questions

1 Was it easy for Betty to get to the village school?
2 How often does she have to train?
3 How long does Betty have to train in the mornings?
4 Can she go back to bed after her morning run?
5 Why can't she go to a lot of late-night parties?
6 What other three things mustn't she do?
7 Is she a sprinter or a long distance runner?
8 What important race has she just won?
9 Did she win easily?
10 What happened after the race?

B Tell the story (1)

Put these sentences in the correct order.

a Then after work she has to go to the gym for more training.
b Betty M'bow grew up in a small African village.
c As well as training hard, she has to be very careful what she eats.
d Since that time her ambition has been to become a top athlete.
e Yesterday she got to her first Olympic final.
f It's a hard life. She has to get up at 5 a.m. to train.
g All the hard training has been worthwhile.
h Then she goes to her job in a hotel.
i She just beat the other seven finalists to win the gold medal.
j She had to go 6 km to the nearest school, so she ran there.
k She does two hours' training and then goes to bed.

C Tell the story (2)

Look at the pictures again. You are Betty. Describe your career. Talk about your childhood, your training programme and way of life, and the big race.

D Guided interview

Interview the manager of the hotel where Betty works.

3 *Yesterday*

4

5

For example: Ask him if she has a full-time job there.
'Does she have a full-time job at the hotel?'
'Yes. She works here six days a week.'

1 Ask him what the hotel guests think about Betty.
2 Ask him if he gives her time off for training and races.
3 Ask him whether the hotel will celebrate her success.
4 Ask him if he will raise her salary because she is famous.

Interview an agent who wants her to sponsor sportswear.

5 Ask him what he wants Betty to do.
6 Ask him what terms he will offer her.
7 Ask him which two world famous sports stars he would like to advertise his products.

E   Task

One student shows any sport in mime (acting without words). Then he/she points to another student, who must say the name of the sport in English. If this is correct, the students both score a point and the name of the sport is written on the blackboard. It is then the turn of the student who guessed correctly to mime a different sport. Continue round the class. How many sports can your class collect in 5 minutes?

F   Writing

Choose any *one* sport or activity which you really enjoy, for example skiing, football, dancing, chess. Write down about five sentences showing the main attractions of the sport or activity.

G   Discussion

Form a small group to fill in the chart below, showing your favourite sports and activities. A 'team sport' or 'group activity' needs a number of people to play or do it, for example hockey or square dancing. An 'individual' sport or activity needs only one person, for example swimming or model making.

	group/team	individual
sport		
activity		

Vaccine

DOCTORS CONQUER SMALLPOX
No new outbreaks since 1976

Killer Disease Eradicated

A VICTORY FOR MEDICAL SCIENCE

2

For thousands of years . . .

3

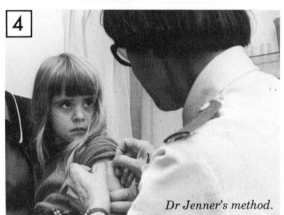

Dr Edward Jenner, discoverer of smallpox vaccine in 1796.

4

Dr Jenner's method.

Vocabulary

Picture 1   a disease, to eradicate, to conquer
      2   smallpox victims
      4   vaccine, a syringe, to inject
      5   outbreaks of disease
      6   a conference, a campaign, a vaccination programme
      7   a medical team
      8   storage, deep freeze

A   Questions

1   What does 'eradicate' mean?
2   Why was smallpox such a serious disease?
3   What important medical discovery was made in 1796?
4   How do doctors vaccinate patients?
5   Why do they do this?
6   What difference had vaccination made by 1900?
7   What did the World Health Organization do in 1965?
8   Why did teams of doctors visit Third World villages?
9   Why is 1976 an important date for medical science?
10   What precautions have been taken against the return of smallpox?

B   Tell the story (1)

_____ science has _____ smallpox. Smallpox is a terrible _____. It has _____ millions of people.

In _____ a British doctor called Edward Jenner _____ a way of protecting people from smallpox. He _____ them with vaccine. This _____ gave them a slight but not serious form of the disease. After vaccination their bodies were able to resist smallpox.

Other countries started to _____ this treatment, and by _____ there was almost no smallpox in _____ _____ or _____. But _____ of smallpox continued in South America, Asia and _____.

In 1965, the _____ _____ _____ began a _____ against smallpox. They started a vaccination _____. Since then, teams of doctors have _____ many villages in the Third World. They have _____ millions of villagers. Now they have _____ the disease. The last _____ was in Africa in 1976. There are huge stores of _____ in _____ and in New Delhi in case of further outbreaks.

Smallpox used to be a serious _____. Now _____ _____ has conquered it.

C   Tell the story (2)

Look at the pictures again. In your own words, give a talk about the problems of smallpox, the importance

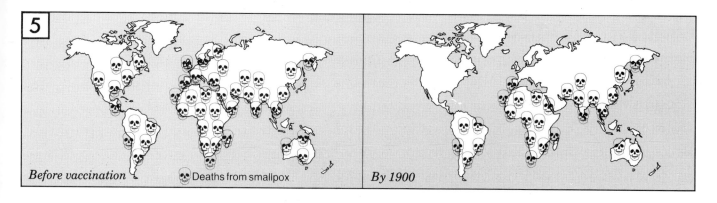

5

Before vaccination   Deaths from smallpox   *By 1900*

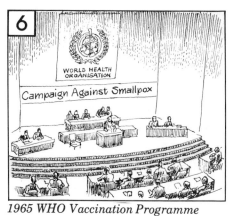

6

WORLD HEALTH ORGANISATION

Campaign Against Smallpox

1965 WHO Vaccination Programme

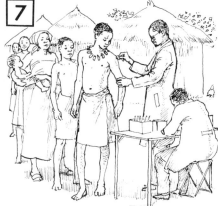

7

8

Last outbreaks:
South America   1971
Asia   1975
Africa   1976
Vaccine for 200
million vaccinations
is stored in Geneva
and New Delhi.

VACCINES

of Jenner's discovery, the effect of the World Health Organization programme, and the precautions against a new outbreak of the disease.

D   Guided interview

The year is 1975. Interview a doctor who is working on a village vaccination programme in East Africa.

For example: Ask her when she started work on the programme.
'When did you start work on the programme?'
'I started work on the programme in 1970.'

1   Ask her how long she has worked in East Africa.
2   Ask about living conditions in the villages.
3   Ask her what is the main difficulty of her work.
4   Ask her what she likes about the job.
5   Ask her how the vaccination programme is going.

E   Task

Work in groups.

You are running an organization which helps poor people in a part of Africa. There is a lot of malnutrition, river blindness and lack of adequate housing. You have raised enough money for *three* of the following projects. Decide which you will choose, and why. Discuss your choice with other groups.

– tinned food for one year
– seed for future crops
– a well-equipped clinic in the largest town
– equipment for irrigation and pumping water
– one thousand temporary shelters, plus blankets and clothing
– two teachers to instruct on reading, writing and hygiene
– a small plane to spray insecticide on swamps

F   Writing

You are a doctor. Write a report of your visit to a remote African village. What health problems did you find there? How did you persuade the suspicious villagers to be vaccinated?

G   Discussion

By accident, your group has discovered a vaccine which prevents people ageing. Anyone you inject with it remains the same age for ever. What will you do with your discovery?

Mother Theresa

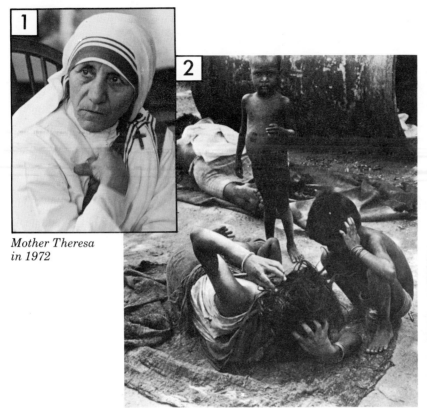

Mother Theresa
in 1972

The poor of Calcutta, who Mother Theresa decided to help.

She founded the 'Sisters of Charity' who go out into the streets everyday.

Vocabulary

Picture 1   a nun
       2   a street scene, the homeless, the destitute, poverty
       3   to found (an organization), a clinic
       4   a temporary shelter, to care for
       5   the Nobel Peace Prize
       6   to hold, to comfort, to feel pity for, an orphan

A   Questions

1 Describe what Mother Theresa looked like in 1972.
2 What are nuns?
3 Where do the Sisters of Charity work?
4 What are conditions like there?
5 Why do the sisters leave their clinic each day?
6 How do they give some comfort to the destitute and dying?
7 What did Mother Theresa receive in 1979?
8 Why did Mother Theresa deserve this?
9 What do you think she did with the large sum of money from the Nobel Foundation?
10 What do you think Mother Theresa felt about the orphan?

B   Tell the story (1)

Mother Theresa first _____ to India in 1929. She _____ to live in Calcutta and work among the _____. She founded the Sisters of _____, a group of _____ whose main job was to _____ for the destitute and dying.

The Sisters run clinics, and _____ temporary shelters on the pavements of Calcutta. Every day, the nuns walk through the _____ of Calcutta, and _____ back people who are ill or nearly dead. They also care for _____, especially orphans.

In 1979, Mother Theresa _____ the Nobel Peace Prize. She accepted it in the name of the _____ and _____ people of the world.

C   Tell the story (2)

Look at the photographs again. You are one of the Sisters of Charity. Describe the conditions in Calcutta. Talk about your work and what you try to do. Describe Mother Theresa and what she has done.

The Sisters build temporary shelters on the Calcutta pavements.

In 1979 Mother Theresa received the Nobel Peace Prize.

In Calcutta her work continues ...

D Guided interview

Interview the chairman of the Nobel Peace Prize committee.

For example: Ask him when he first heard of the work of Mother Theresa.
'When did you first hear of the work of Mother Theresa?'
'I first heard about her work in the early seventies.'

1 Ask him for three reasons why his committee gave the Prize to Mother Theresa.
2 Ask him to describe the prize-giving ceremony.
3 Ask him about Mother Theresa's reaction to the award and what she said at the ceremony.
4 Ask him what he thinks Mother Theresa will do with the prize money.
5 Ask him what he thought of Mother Theresa as a person.

E Task

Form a group to organize a local fund-raising event to collect £500 for Mother Theresa's work in Calcutta.

This event could be a sponsored walk, swim or run, a lottery or second-hand sale, a door-to-door collection, or some other idea.

Work out – what the event will be
          – who you will need (e.g. volunteers, police)
          – what you will need (e.g. tickets, prizes)
          – where you will hold the event.

Explain your ideas to the other groups.

F Writing

Write a description of picture 4. What sort of place is it? Who are the people? What are they wearing? What are they doing?

G Discussion

Mother Theresa is a most remarkable woman. Discuss other great or famous women in world history.
Produce a list headed 'The world's six greatest women of all time', and give reasons for your choices.

Campers

Vocabulary

Picture 1   to lean on, a gate
       2   to push, a roof-rack, to go camping, a warning notice, to run out of petrol
       3   a picnic basket, empty
       4   a fishing rod, to get soaked, to put up a tent, to unload
       5   to attack, to tear, barbed wire
       7   to collapse

A   Questions

1   Are the two farmers worried about the campers or are they amused by them?
2   In picture 2, why are the family pushing their car?
3   Why did they push it into the field?
4   What didn't they see?
5   They might have forgotten the picnic. Can you think of another reason why the basket is empty?
6   Why is the boy so wet?
7   Why did they need a first aid box?
8   What happened in the night?
9   Mrs Thompson must have got some petrol – where from?
10   What are Mr Thompson and the children going to do next?

B   Tell the story (1)

Complete the dialogue. In your answers, use 'must have', 'might have', or 'going to'.

Farmer Brown:	I wonder what's happened.
Farmer Giles:	They ... (picture 2)
Farmer Brown:	I wonder what they're going to do now.
Farmer Giles:	I think they ... (picture 2)
Farmer Brown:	Now what's the trouble?
Farmer Giles:	I think the boy ... (picture 3)
Farmer Brown:	I wonder what they ... for supper.
Farmer Giles:	They're probably ...
Farmer Brown:	Now what's happened?
Farmer Giles:	The boy ... (picture 4)
Farmer Brown:	More trouble! The father has torn his trousers.
Farmer Giles:	Yes, your bull ... or he ... them on the barbed wire. (picture 5)
Farmer Brown:	I wonder what they're going to do next!
Farmer Giles:	I expect ...

C   Tell the story (2)

Look at the pictures again. You are the small boy. Tell the story of your camping holiday. Describe everything that went wrong. Say how you eventually got home.

D   Guided interview

Two of the class are Mr and Mrs Thompson. Ask them about the camping holiday.

40

For example: Ask them what equipment they took
and how they carried it.
'What equipment did you take and how
did you carry it?'
'We took a tent and various other
things and carried them on the roof of
the car.'

1   Ask them why they decided to camp in that
particular field.
2   Ask them why their son went fishing and what
happened.
3   Ask them what else went wrong that evening.
4   Ask them if they had a comfortable night in the
tent.
5   Ask them about their holiday plans for next year.

You have invented the super safari tent in the
picture. It includes the following special features:

a bicycle   a camouflaged periscope
a platform   spears
a magnifying glass   a fan
a spit for cooking   a bucket

Write a short advertisement for the super safari tent
explaining how the lucky owner –

a   moves from one place to another in the tent
b   can observe wild animals without being seen
c   defends himself against attack
d   collects water
e   cooks
f   keeps insects away

E Task

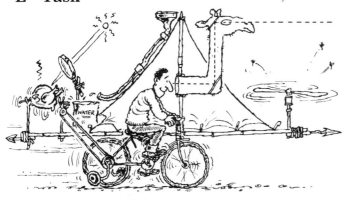

The Super Safari tent.

F Writing

The Thompsons' camping holiday has led to a major
family row. Write down *either* Mr Thompson's version
of what happened, *or* Mrs Thompson's version.

G Discussion

Do you think camping is a good way to spend a
holiday? Discuss camping holidays you have been on,
or ones that your friends have told you about. What
are the main advantages and disadvantages of
camping?

Balloon Flight

Vocabulary

Picture 1 a newsreader, a hot-air balloon, to set off, balloonists

2 a weather chart, a storm, thunder and lightning, the Alps

3 to crash, to search, a rescue, helicopters

4 a mountain rescue team, a stretcher, a first aid kit, to be injured

5 to lift to safety

6 a hospital ward, to break a leg, to recover, to feel much better, to plan

A Questions

1 What were the two balloonists trying to do?
2 Describe the balloon.
3 What was the weather like over the mountains?
4 What happened to the balloon?
5 How did the rescue team reach them?
6 What equipment did the rescue team take with them?
7 Why were Claude and Raymond taken off the mountainside by helicopter?
8 How badly injured were they?
9 What are their plans for the future?
10 How did the newscaster's expression change as he gave the bulletins?

B Tell the story (1)

Arrange these sentences in the correct order.

a Rescue helicopters searched a wide area.
b The takeoff was watched by large crowds.
c The mountain rescue team reached the balloonists.
d They gave the balloonists first aid.
e In hospital, Claude and Raymond seemed cheerful.
f Last week, two balloonists attempted to fly from Paris to Rome.
g They sighted the crashed balloonists and radioed the mountain rescue team.
h The rescue helicopter took them to hospital.
i They said they had plans for a longer flight next year.
j That night heavy thunderstorms were reported over the Alps.

C Tell the story (2)

Look at the pictures again. Prepare a series of six news bulletins (one for each picture) covering the story. Describe the events in each picture as if they have just happened. Begin each bulletin 'Here is the latest news . . .' For example: 'Here is the latest news. Two French balloonists have just taken off from . . .'

D Guided interview

Two of the class are Claude and Raymond. Ask them about the flight.

For example: Ask them why they wanted to make the flight from Paris to Rome.
'Why did you want to make the flight from Paris to Rome?'
'We thought it would be exciting.'

1 Ask them about the start of the flight.
2 Ask them what happened over the Alps.
3 Ask them what their injuries were.
4 Ask them how they were rescued.
5 Ask them how they are feeling now.
6 Ask them if they have any plans for future balloon trips and, if so, how they will make them safer.

E Task

You are going on a balloon flight. From the list below, choose the *five* most important things to take with you: binoculars, chocolate, an electric razor, a map, an interesting book, a tape recorder and cassettes, warm clothes, a toothbrush, a star guide, a camera, a pack of cards, a torch, suntan oil, a first aid kit, signal rockets.
Compare your list of items around the class. Give reasons for each choice.

F Writing

Write a short story about a balloon flight. Mention each of your five items (from the Task) in the story.

G Discussion

Form a small group to discuss which is the best sport – ballooning, hang gliding, surfing or skiing. To help you decide, fill in the table below. Give each sport a mark out of 10 for each of the columns. Add up the totals and put the sports in order, beginning with the one which has the highest marks.

	exciting	cheap	easy to do	needs little equipment
ballooning				
hang gliding				
surfing				
skiing				
totals				

The Microchip Revolution

Silicon chips.

1960 $5,000,000   1980 $5,000

Some uses now ...

Uses in industry.

Vocabulary

Picture 1 a microchip (a silicon chip), an electronic circuit
  2 a computer, a microcomputer
  3 a pocket calculator, a digital watch, a body scanner, a screen
  4 automation, a robot
  6 a talking computer
  7 unemployment, the Third World, less developed countries

A Questions

1 What are microchips made of?
2 How big are they?
3 How have microchips affected the design of computers?
4 What things are microchips used in at present?
5 How are microchips used in industry?
6 What changes will they make to shopping?
7 What changes will they make in education?
8 What developments are likely in the future?
9 What problems may microchips cause in developed countries?
10 Will advanced technology help the less developed countries?

B Tell the story (1)

Ten sentences have each been split into two halves. Find the correct halves (one from each group) and write the sentences out.

1 A microchip may be held
2 Microchips are made
3 They are small and
4 At present they are used in
5 Soon many production processes
6 More and more routine jobs will be
7 Perhaps this will cause
8 By 1990
9 They will
10 The next few years will bring important changes

a inexpensive.
b make a lot of jobs easier.
c will be controlled by computers.
d done by robots.
e of silicon.
f in our life style.
g there will be many home computers.
h between your finger and thumb.
i massive unemployment.
j computers and microcomputers.

How will the microchip change our daily lives?

Future developments.

Will everyone benefit?

C Tell the story (2)

Look at the pictures again. Explain what a microchip is. How important is it at present? How has it changed industry and daily life? What future changes do you expect?

D Guided interview

Interview one or two other students in the class. Ask them questions to find out which of the ideas below they think:

a *will happen* by the year 2001.
b *may happen* by the year 2001.
c *won't happen* by the year 2001.

1 There will be advanced computers in most Western homes.
2 Most factories will be manned by robots.
3 Computers will have replaced doctors.
4 There won't be any schools or colleges: all learning will be done in the home.
5 There will be very few shops: ordering and delivery will be arranged by computer.
6 All voting will be done on computer keyboards.
7 Most people will have videophones, so they can see and hear the person they are phoning.
8 Everyone will have much more spare time than they do now.
9 Handwriting will no longer be taught to children.

E Task

You are the sales director of a large computer firm. Think of two developments in each of the following areas where computers will bring changes:

a medicine
b personal transport systems
c education
d domestic: homes and gardens
e personal communications systems

Pick out the three developments which you think will be most important for your firm.

F Writing

List ten things which are usually done by people at the present, but which will be done by machines in the year 2001. Write an explanation for any two changes you mention on your list.

G Discussion

By the end of the century, many more people will be unemployed. Others will do their work entirely at home, using computers. Advanced computers will play an increasing part in our lives – but only a few skilled scientists will understand how they work. Does this view of the future worry you, or excite you? Or do you believe it won't happen like that?

The Temples That Were Moved

Temples stood at Philae for over two thousand years.

In 1970 the Egyptian government constructed the Aswan High Dam across the Nile.

The new water level damaged the ancient temples.

Vocabulary

Picture 2 a temple, to build, a column, a statue
    3 a dam, electricity
    4 to be flooded, water level, to erode, a carving
    5 a coffer dam, to construct
    6 a stone block, to measure, to number, to take to pieces, to transport
    7 an island, to reconstruct
    8 to complete a project, a tourist attraction

A Questions

1 Where were the temples built?
2 Who built them – and when?
3 Describe the temples.
4 Why do you think the Aswan High Dam was built?
5 What effect did this have on the river Nile?
6 In what way were the temples in danger?
7 What did UNESCO and the Egyptian Government decide to do?
8 What was the coffer dam (picture 5) for?
9 Why was each block numbered? (picture 6)
10 Why do you think the island of Agilkia (picture 7) is a good site for the rebuilt temples?

B Tell the story (1)

The temples at Philae were _____ in the fourth century BC. In 1970, the Aswan High Dam was constructed. It was needed to provide _____ for hydroelectricity and irrigation. The Dam made the water level of the Nile _____ and so most of the Philae temples _____ _____.

The Egyptian government and UNESCO got together and _____ $16 million to save the temples. First a coffer dam _____ _____. Each _____ of the temples was numbered and then it was _____ to the nearby island of Agilkia. This island was _____ the high water level. Here the temples would be _____.

This great and imaginative task _____ _____ in 1980. Most of the stonework and _____ are undamaged, so _____ can get a good idea of the original beauty of the _____.

C Tell the story (2)

You are the director of the operation that saved the temples.

Explain – why you started the project.
        – where the money came from.

46

The start of rescue work by UNESCO and the Egyptian government.

Each stone block was carefully numbered and removed.

A new site for the temples on the island of Agilkia.

1980: the rescue is completed.

- how the coffer dam was built.
- how the 40,000 stones were numbered.
- how they were transported to Agilkia.
- what problems your team came across.
- what the temples now look like.
- why you think the project was worthwhile.

D Guided interview

Interview an archaeologist who has worked in Egypt. Ask him about the Philae temples.

For example: Ask him if they are very important.
'Are the temples very important?'
'Oh, yes. Even though they were built over two thousand years ago they are still in good condition.'

1   Ask him if he knows who built them – and why.
2   Ask him how badly they were damaged by the Nile.
3   Ask him what can be seen at the new site.
4   Ask him if he thinks the rebuilt temples will be visited by a lot of tourists.
5   Ask him if there are other temples still waiting to be discovered.

E Task

Produce a serious sounding plan for moving a famous building, for example the Leaning Tower of Pisa, the Statue of Liberty, or the Great Wall of China, to a new site. Give reasons for the move and for the choice of new site. Include details of how the building will be moved.

For example: the roar of London traffic drowns the chimes of Big Ben, which must be moved to the North Pole where there are fewer cars. Big Ben will be dismantled and transported on giant barges, and then dog-teams will pull the blocks of stone across the ice . . .

F Writing

Give an eyewitness account of one dramatic moment during the Great Move (see the Task).

G Discussion

Is it right to spend huge sums of money on preserving old temples when millions of the world's poor are starving?

We are grateful to the following for permission to reproduce copyright photographs:

Alan Band Associates for page 44 (top left); Barnaby's Picture Library for pages 12 (top right) & 23 (middle); BBC Hulton Picture Library for pages 22 (left), 22 (right), 23 (left) & 36 (bottom left); Camera Press Ltd. for pages 23 (right), 31 & 46 (bottom left); Camera Press Ltd./ photo by S.K. Dutt for pages 38 (middle), 38 (right), 39 (left) & 39 (right); J. Allan Cash Ltd. for page 13 (top right); Central Electricity Generating Board for page 30 (bottom left); Fiat Auto (U.K.) Ltd. for page 44 (bottom right); Hong Kong Government Office for page 13 (top left); John Topham Picture Library for pages 14 (top right), 14 (bottom right), 15 (top left), 15 (bottom left) & 22 (middle); Keystone Press Agency Ltd. for page 39 (middle); Rex Features Ltd. for pages 15 (right) & 30 (bottom right); Robert Harding Picture Library for page 28 (top left); Susan Griggs Agency Ltd. for page 14 (left); Syndication International Ltd. for pages 36 (bottom right) & 38 (left); UNESCO for pages 46 (middle left), 46 (right) & 47; Zefa Picture Library (U.K.) Ltd. for page 12 (bottom right).

Illustrations by Oxford Illustrators, David Parkins, Gay Galsworthy and John Fraser.

Cover photographs by: BBC Hulton Picture Library (bottom middle); Camera Press Ltd. (top middle right); UNESCO (top left).